# SUMMARY OF HIDDEN MYSTERIES AND THE BIBLE

*Secrets Revealed: Aliens/UFOs, Giants, Time Travel, Multiverse, AI, and Other Unexplained Phenomena*

## LARRY OLLISON

Copyright 2024–Harrison House

All rights reserved. This book is protected by the copyright laws of the United States of America. This book may not be copied or reprinted for commercial gain or profit. The use of short quotations or occasional page copying for personal or group study is permitted and encouraged. Permission will be granted upon request. Unless otherwise indicated, all scripture quotations are taken from the *King James Version* of the Bible. Used by permission. All rights reserved.

All emphasis within Scripture quotations is the author's own. Please note that Harrison House's publishing style capitalizes certain pronouns in Scripture that refer to the Father, Son, and Holy Spirit, and may differ from some publishers' styles. Take note that the name satan and related names are not capitalized. We choose not to acknowledge him, even to the point of violating grammatical rules.

Harrison House P.O. Box 310, Shippensburg, PA 17257-0310

This book and all other Harrison House's books are available at Christian bookstores and distributors worldwide.

For Worldwide Distribution.

Reach us on the Internet: www.harrisonhouse.com.

ISBN 13 TP: 9781667508870

ISBN 13 eBook: 9781667508887

# CONTENTS

| | |
|---|---:|
| Introduction | v |
| 1. Are We Alone? | 1 |
| 2. In the Beginning | 5 |
| 3. The World Before Adam and Eve | 9 |
| 4. The Watchers and the Nephilim | 12 |
| 5. Who Built the Ancient Structures? | 16 |
| 6. Angels of God | 20 |
| 7. UFOs and the Bible | 23 |
| 8. Time Travel | 27 |
| 9. Artificial Intelligence and the Coming Apocalypse | 31 |
| 10. Transhumanism, Cryonics, and Eternal Life | 35 |
| 11. Flat Earth Theory | 39 |
| 12. Ghosts | 42 |
| 13. What Is the Multiverse? | 46 |
| 14. Climate Change | 50 |
| 15. Heaven, Hell, and Eternity | 54 |
| 16. The Mystery of the Hebrew Language | 58 |
| About the Publisher | 63 |

# INTRODUCTION

❧

The Bible is a profound and intricate book, revered for its spiritual guidance and historical significance. However, beyond its surface lies a tapestry of hidden mysteries and deeper meanings waiting to be unveiled. This summary explores the multifaceted dimensions of the Bible, focusing on its prophetic nature, the unique characteristics of the Hebrew language, and the divine codes embedded within the Scriptures. By delving into these hidden mysteries, we uncover the extraordinary ways in which God's messages are intricately woven into the text, offering believers a richer, more profound understanding of His eternal plan.

# CHAPTER 1

# ARE WE ALONE?

**Bible Verse**
"For the Spirit searches all things, yes, the deep things of God." - 1 Corinthians 2:10

**Introduction**

The age-old question of whether humanity is alone in the universe is explored through various perspectives, including science, theology, and personal reflection. This chapter delves into the complexities of the cosmos, the nature of intelligent design, and the spiritual insights offered by the Bible.

**Word of Wisdom**

*"It is ludicrous to think that everything we see is a result of the miraculous rearranging of space dust. We must ac-*

*knowledge this: We are not alone." Larry Ollison*

## Main Theme

The exploration of whether humanity is alone in the universe, considering scientific, philosophical, and theological perspectives, ultimately pointing to the existence of an intelligent designer.

## Key Points

- Ellie Arroway's childhood wonder in "Contact" encapsulates humanity's quest to know if we are alone.
- Advances in science and technology raise more questions than answers about the universe.
- Prominent scientists recognize an intelligence behind the universe's complexity, even if they deny traditional religious views.
- The vastness of the universe and the intricacies of life suggest a higher intelligence at work.
- The Bible provides insights and answers that align with the concept of intelligent design.
- The enduring mysteries of the universe find coherence in the wisdom of the Holy Scriptures.

## Key Themes

- **Scientific and Theological Inquiry:** The chapter intertwines scientific discoveries with theological insights, presenting a balanced view of the quest for understanding the universe and our place in it.
- **Intelligent Design:** Despite the denial of a personal deity by some scientists, the chapter argues for an intelligent design, suggesting that the complexity of the universe points to a higher power.
- **Human Limitations:** By comparing human understanding to a child's comprehension, the chapter emphasizes the limitations of human intellect in grasping the full scope of divine wisdom.
- **The Role of the Bible:** The chapter highlights the Bible as a source of ultimate truth and guidance, offering answers to profound questions about existence and creation.
- **Existence of Multiple Dimensions:** It discusses the possibility of multiple dimensions and unseen worlds, reinforcing the idea that what we see is just a fraction of reality.

## Conclusion

Humanity is not alone in the vast universe. The intricate design and order of creation point to an intelligent designer, which the Bible reveals as God. This recognition bridges the gap between scientific discovery and spiritual wisdom, affirming that we are part of a greater plan and purpose.

## CHAPTER 2

## IN THE BEGINNING

### Bible Verse

"But you, Daniel, shut up the words, and seal the book until the time of the end; many shall run to and fro, and knowledge shall increase." - Daniel 12:4

### Introduction

This chapter explores the differing views on the creation of the world from both a scientific and a biblical perspective, emphasizing the harmony between true science and the Bible. It discusses the concepts of Young Earth and Old Earth Creationism, the role of intelligent design, and the importance of aligning our understanding with the Word of God.

### Word of Wisdom

*"Scientific facts change, but the ab-*

*solute foundational truth in the Word of God never changes." Larry Ollison*

## Main Theme

The chapter examines the origins of the universe and humanity from both conservative and progressive Christian viewpoints, emphasizing the enduring truth of the Bible amidst evolving scientific theories.

## Key Points

- The author's conservative Christian upbringing instilled a deep trust in the Bible's accuracy.
- Science and the Bible are not in conflict; true scientific discoveries confirm biblical truths.
- The Holy Spirit reveals deeper understanding of Scripture as we approach the end times.
- There are two primary views on creation: Young Earth and Old Earth Creationism.
- The term "Bara Elohim" indicates that the Trinity was involved in creation.
- Genesis provides an overview of creation, which can be interpreted in various ways.

## Key Themes

- **Young Earth vs. Old Earth Creationism:** Young Earth Creationists believe the universe was created in six literal 24-hour days, while Old Earth Creationists interpret the creation account as spanning a longer period. Both views affirm divine design.
- **Role of the Holy Spirit:** The Holy Spirit, given to the church after Jesus' ascension, plays a crucial role in revealing the truths hidden in Scripture, especially in the end times, as knowledge increases.
- **Scientific Insights:** Historical figures like George Washington Carver illustrate how scientific discoveries can align with and confirm biblical truths, demonstrating that science and faith are not mutually exclusive.
- **Genesis and Creation:** The first chapter of Genesis serves as an overview of creation, with the phrase "God created" (Bara Elohim) indicating the involvement of the Trinity in the creation process.
- **Literal vs. Allegorical Interpretation:** The chapter addresses debates about whether Adam and Eve were real individuals or symbolic representations, affirming their literal existence as foundational to Christian faith.

## Conclusion

The creation of the universe and humanity is a profound topic that bridges science and theology.

Understanding the different perspectives on creation helps us appreciate the harmony between the Bible and scientific discoveries. Ultimately, the truth of God's Word remains unchanging and provides a foundation for our faith and understanding of the world.

## CHAPTER 3

# THE WORLD BEFORE ADAM AND EVE

**Bible Verse**
"In hope of eternal life which God, who cannot lie, promised before time began." - Titus 1:2

**Introduction**

This chapter delves into the concept of a pre-Adamic world, exploring scientific and biblical perspectives on the creation and the ancient history of the earth. It examines the nature of the universe, the fall of Lucifer, and the evidence for civilizations existing before Adam and Eve.

**Word of Wisdom**

*"Do not allow your view of creation to separate you from your brothers and sisters in the body of Christ and keep you from walking in love." Larry Ollison*

## Main Theme

The chapter explores the idea of a pre-Adamic world, considering scientific theories and biblical accounts to understand the state of the universe before the creation of Adam and Eve.

## Key Points

- Belief in a pre-Adamic civilization does not affect one's salvation.
- Scientists believe the universe began with a singularity and expanded rapidly.
- The Hubble and James Webb telescopes have expanded our understanding of the universe.
- The Bible describes the earth as initially perfect but later becoming formless and void due to Lucifer's fall.
- The concept of time was created by God, who existed before time began.
- Two distinct floods are described in the Bible: the Luciferian flood and Noah's flood.

## Key Themes

- **Scientific View of Creation:** The leading scientific explanation suggests the universe began with a massive explosion and expanded rapidly. As technology advances, our understanding of the universe continues to grow.
- **Lucifer's Fall:** Lucifer, originally a perfect cherub, led a rebellion against God and was cast down to earth, causing chaos

and destruction. This led to the first flood, which left the earth formless and void.
- **Biblical Evidence of Pre-Adamic Civilizations:** Scriptures such as Isaiah and Ezekiel provide insights into the existence of kingdoms and civilizations before Adam and Eve. These beings engaged in commerce and were led by Lucifer.
- **Two Floods:** The chapter distinguishes between the Luciferian flood, which destroyed the earth's original perfection, and Noah's flood, which was a judgment on human sin and angelic corruption. Both events reshaped the earth.
- **God's Eternal Existence:** God existed before time began and created everything with a purpose. The Bible emphasizes the eternal nature of God and His unchanging plan for creation.

## Conclusion

The concept of a world before Adam and Eve provides a deeper understanding of the Bible's account of creation and the fall of Lucifer. While interpretations may vary, the central truth remains that God's Word offers a coherent explanation of the universe's origins and His eternal plan. Embracing this knowledge enriches our faith and highlights the grandeur of God's creation.

## CHAPTER 4

# THE WATCHERS AND THE NEPHILIM

### Bible Verse

"For if God did not spare the angels who sinned, but cast them down to hell and delivered them into chains of darkness, to be reserved for judgment; and did not spare the ancient world, but saved Noah, one of eight people, a preacher of righteousness, bringing in the flood on the world of the ungodly." - 2 Peter 2:4-5

### Introduction

This chapter explores the biblical and historical accounts of the Watchers and the Nephilim, angelic beings who took human wives and produced giants. This event, combined with human perversion, led to the flood in Noah's time.

### Word of Wisdom

*"Your belief about creation is not*

*salvation critical. Do not allow your view of creation to separate you from your brothers and sisters in the body of Christ and keep you from walking in love." Larry Ollison*

## Main Theme

The chapter examines the interactions between angels and humans that resulted in the Nephilim, exploring the implications of these events on human history and divine judgment.

## Key Points

- The "sons of God" in Genesis 6 are widely interpreted as angels who took human wives and bore giants, known as Nephilim.
- The Book of Job supports the interpretation of the "sons of God" as angels present at creation.
- The Sethite view, which claims the "sons of God" were human descendants of Seth, is historically and logically flawed.
- The New Testament differentiates between Old Testament "sons of God" (angels) and New Testament "sons of God" (believers).
- Two groups of angels sinned: those who fell with Lucifer and the Watchers who took human wives.
- The Watchers are imprisoned in Tartarus, awaiting judgment for their transgressions.

## Key Themes

- **Historical and Biblical Evidence:** The chapter highlights the consistency across various ancient texts, including the Book of Enoch and the writings of early church fathers, affirming that the "sons of God" were angels.
- **The Nature of the Watchers:** These specific angels were assigned to oversee humanity but chose to sin by taking human wives, resulting in a distorted offspring, the Nephilim, who caused chaos and violence on earth.
- **Genetic Perversion and Judgment:** The union between the Watchers and human women led to the corruption of human DNA, which necessitated the flood to preserve the possibility of a perfect sacrificial Lamb, Jesus Christ.
- **New Testament Context:** The chapter clarifies that New Testament references to "sons of God" pertain to believers, while Old Testament references pertain to angels, distinguishing between their roles and identities.
- **Purpose of the Flood:** The flood was an act of divine love to eliminate the corrupted genetics of the Nephilim, ensuring the future possibility of redemption through Jesus Christ.

## Conclusion

The chapter underscores the importance of understanding these ancient events to grasp the depth of God's plan for redemption. Despite the chaos caused by the Watchers and Nephilim, God's intervention through the flood was an act of love to preserve humanity and pave the way for the ultimate sacrifice of Jesus Christ.

## CHAPTER 5

# WHO BUILT THE ANCIENT STRUCTURES?

**Bible Verse**

"There were giants on the earth in those days, and also afterward..." - Genesis 6:4

**Introduction**

This chapter explores the mysterious and ancient structures found across the globe, questioning who built them, how they were constructed with such precision, and where the builders acquired their advanced knowledge and skills. The chapter delves into the possibility of non-human involvement in these constructions.

**Word of Wisdom**

*"Understanding who built the ancient structures requires a deep study of Scripture and sometimes unlearning previous beliefs to uncover the ultimate truth."*
*Larry Ollison*

## Main Theme

The chapter investigates the origins and builders of ancient megalithic structures, considering the involvement of ancient civilizations, giants, and potentially non-human beings, in light of biblical chronology and archaeological evidence.

## Key Points

- Ancient structures worldwide exhibit a level of precision and complexity that modern technology struggles to replicate.
- The Hypogeum in Malta, an underground palace, contains acoustically engineered rooms and was discovered with elongated skulls and artifacts.
- Ġgantija, the second oldest temple on the planet, was built with massive stones and is linked to legends of giants.
- Göbekli Tepe in Türkiye, predating Stonehenge, features massive T-shaped limestone megaliths with intricate carvings.
- The Sphinx of Giza and the Great Pyramids of Egypt showcase advanced engineering and construction techniques unexplained by current historical understanding.
- Structures like Newgrange in Ireland align with celestial bodies, indicating advanced astronomical knowledge.

## Key Themes

- **Mysterious Construction Techniques:** Many ancient structures, such as the Hypogeum and Ġgantija, were built with precision and massive stones, raising questions about the technology and methods used by their builders.
- **Legends and Giants:** Folklore and legends, like those surrounding Ġgantija, often involve giants and suggest that these beings may have played a role in the construction of ancient structures.
- **Advanced Knowledge and Skills:** Sites like Göbekli Tepe and Newgrange reveal a deep understanding of astronomy, geometry, and engineering far beyond what is typically attributed to ancient agrarian societies.
- **Biblical and Archaeological Correlation:** The chapter correlates biblical accounts, such as the existence of giants and ancient civilizations, with archaeological findings to propose that non-human entities may have contributed to these constructions.
- **Timeline and Civilization:** By examining the timeline from the original creation to post-flood periods, the chapter posits that different beings, including angels, giants, and early humans, could have been responsible for building these ancient structures.

## Conclusion

Determining who built the ancient structures requires considering biblical timelines and archaeological evidence. Structures built after Noah's flood were likely constructed by humans, potentially with the assistance of Nephilim. Structures predating Adam's expulsion from Eden could have been built by ancient non-human civilizations and angels. A thorough study of Scripture, alongside archaeological discoveries, is essential to uncover the true builders of these ancient wonders.

## CHAPTER 6

## ANGELS OF GOD

### Bible Verse

"Are they not all ministering spirits sent forth to minister for those who will inherit salvation?" - Hebrews 1:14

### Introduction

This chapter delves into the existence, purpose, and activities of angels according to the Bible. It aims to clarify misconceptions and provide an accurate understanding of angels based on scriptural references.

### Word of Wisdom

*"Angels are here to assist Christians, and Christians have been given authority over the devil and his fallen angels." Larry Ollison*

## Main Theme

The chapter explores the creation, roles, and significance of angels in the spiritual realm, emphasizing their interactions with humans and their place in God's plan.

## Key Points

- Angels were created by God before humans and serve specific purposes, including worship and delivering messages.
- There are different rankings among angels, such as archangels, seraphim, and cherubim.
- Angels have not always existed; they were created at a specific point in time.
- Two main groups of angels exist today: the loyal angels of God and the fallen angels who followed Lucifer.
- Angels can alter their appearance and intervene in human affairs as messengers and protectors.
- Christians should communicate with God through Jesus, not directly seek interactions with angels.

## Key Themes

- **Creation and Purpose of Angels:**
  Angels were created by God to worship Him and serve as messengers. They exist in different rankings and were created before humans.

- **Angels as Messengers:** Throughout history, angels have delivered important messages from God to humans, such as Gabriel's announcements to Zechariah, Mary, and Joseph.
- **Power and Intervention:** Angels possess immense power and can intervene in human affairs, as seen when one angel killed 185,000 Assyrian soldiers in one night.
- **Biblical Examples:** The chapter recounts several biblical stories of angelic intervention, including the blinding of men in Sodom, the protection of Daniel in the lions' den, and the rescue of Peter from prison.
- **Angels in the End Times:** During the Great Tribulation, angels will play a significant role in preaching the gospel and proclaiming God's judgment, demonstrating their ongoing involvement in God's plan.

## Conclusion

Angels are integral to God's plan, serving as messengers and protectors for those who inherit salvation. They have been present throughout biblical history and continue to influence the spiritual realm. Christians are encouraged to recognize the role of angels while maintaining their primary communication with God through Jesus Christ. The existence and activities of angels underscore God's love and provision for His people.

## CHAPTER 7

## UFOS AND THE BIBLE

**Bible Verse**
"Put on the whole armor of God, that you may be able to stand against the wiles of the devil." - Ephesians 6:11

**Introduction**

This chapter explores the intriguing and often controversial topic of unidentified flying objects (UFOs) and their possible connections to the spiritual realm as described in the Bible. It aims to provide a biblical perspective on the phenomenon and address the growing public interest and speculation surrounding UFO sightings and encounters.

**Word of Wisdom**

*"Do not be afraid of a UFO. If a little Grey alien appears to you, do not say, 'Take me to your leader!' Instead say, 'I*

*rebuke you in the name of Jesus!"" Larry Ollison*

## Main Theme

The chapter investigates the phenomenon of UFOs, examining their nature, origins, and the potential for spiritual deception, while offering a biblical explanation for their existence and activity.

## Key Points

• The first movie about space travel, "A Trip to the Moon," was released in 1902, sparking public interest in extraterrestrial life.

• The U.S. government has disclosed reports on UFOs, confirming their existence but not their origins.

• The term "UFO" has evolved to "UAP" (Unidentified Anomalous Phenomena) to include objects entering oceans.

• The Bible provides a framework for understanding spiritual beings and their interactions with the physical world.

• Modern media and government disclosures are desensitizing the public to the idea of extraterrestrial life.

• Discerning spirits is crucial for Christians to avoid deception from fallen angels posing as extraterrestrial beings.

## Key Themes

- **Government Disclosure:** Recent U.S. government disclosures confirm the existence of UFOs, shifting the conversation from fiction to reality. These objects exhibit capabilities beyond human technology, suggesting non-human origins.
- **Biblical Perspective:** The Bible describes encounters with unidentified objects and beings, such as Ezekiel's vision of the wheel within a wheel and the chariots of fire, which can be interpreted as ancient descriptions of UFO-like phenomena.
- **Spiritual Deception:** The Bible warns against deception by fallen angels who can masquerade as benevolent beings. Christians must use discernment to differentiate between God's angels and demonic spirits.
- **Historical and Modern Sightings:** Throughout history, there have been reports and artistic depictions of unexplained aerial phenomena. Today, these sightings continue, with modern technology providing more evidence and documentation.
- **Faith vs. Fear:** Christians are encouraged to respond to UFO phenomena with faith, not fear. The power of faith activates God's angels, while fear empowers demonic spirits. Believers should rely on the Word of God and the authority of Jesus Christ to navigate these experiences.

## Conclusion

The chapter concludes that while UFOs are real and their sightings are increasing, they are best understood through a biblical lens. These phenomena may be manifestations of spiritual beings, and Christians must exercise discernment and faith, avoiding fear and deception. The ultimate truth and protection come from understanding and applying God's Word.

## CHAPTER 8

## TIME TRAVEL

**Bible Verse**

"See then that you walk circumspectly, not as fools but as wise, redeeming the time, because the days are evil." - Ephesians 5:15-16

**Introduction**

This chapter delves into the fascinating concept of time travel, exploring its portrayal in science fiction and its feasibility in real science. It examines how modern physics, particularly Einstein's theory of relativity, reshapes our understanding of time and its implications for humanity.

**Word of Wisdom**

*"God existed before the creation of time because He created it."* Larry Ollison

## Main Theme

The chapter explores the scientific and biblical perspectives on time travel, highlighting the complexity and variability of time, and emphasizing that while physical time travel may be impossible for humans, God exists beyond time and can intervene in miraculous ways.

## Key Points

- Time is a variable, not a constant, and it can be influenced by speed and gravity.

- Einstein's theory of relativity demonstrates that time slows down as speed increases.

- Black holes have a gravitational pull that affects time, showcasing the relationship between gravity and time.

- Scientific experiments have shown that time variation is a real phenomenon.

- Viewing past events through telescopes or recordings is not time travel but an observation of history.

- The Bible suggests that God can alter time and intervene in the timeline of humanity.

## Key Themes

- **Einstein's Relativity:** Einstein's theory of relativity links time and space, showing

that as objects move faster, they experience time more slowly. This theory is supported by experiments involving atomic clocks and GPS technology.
- **Biblical Time Manipulation:** The Bible recounts events like Joshua's command to the sun to stand still, illustrating God's ability to alter time for His purposes. These instances show God's sovereignty over time and space.
- **Prophetic Visions:** Biblical prophets like John and Daniel received visions of the future, not through physical time travel but through divine revelation. These visions provided a glimpse into God's future plans without altering the present timeline.
- **Scientific Impossibility:** Despite advancements in science, time travel remains a theoretical impossibility for humans. The laws of physics and current technology do not support the concept of moving through time as depicted in fiction.
- **God's Eternal Nature:** God exists independently of time, seeing the end from the beginning. He can insert Himself into any point in time, guiding humanity according to His divine plan and foreknowledge.

## Conclusion

While time travel captivates the imagination, it remains beyond human reach according to current scientific understanding. The Bible, however, reveals a God who transcends time, capable of miraculous interventions. Christians are encouraged to trust in God's eternal perspective and redeem the time they have, knowing that God controls the timeline of history.

# CHAPTER 9

# ARTIFICIAL INTELLIGENCE AND THE COMING APOCALYPSE

## Bible Verse

"But you, Daniel, shut up the words, and seal the book until the time of the end; many shall run to and fro, and knowledge shall increase." - Daniel 12:4

## Introduction

This chapter explores the rapid advancement of artificial intelligence (AI) and its potential implications for humanity, especially in the context of biblical prophecy and the coming apocalypse. It reflects on the profound changes in technology from the author's childhood to the present day, emphasizing the exponential growth in knowledge and travel prophesied in the book of Daniel.

## Word of Wisdom

*"Artificial intelligence is merely an advanced program, and every program has a programmer."* Larry Ollison

## Main Theme

The chapter examines the potential dangers and ethical concerns surrounding AI, highlighting its rapid development, potential misuse by malevolent forces, and its possible role in the end times as foretold in biblical prophecy.

## Key Points

• AI has evolved from basic technology to complex systems capable of mimicking human behavior.

• Human intelligence, a gift from God, is inherently superior to artificial intelligence.

• AI lacks moral guidance and is limited by its programming.

• The potential for AI to be misused by malevolent forces, including the antichrist, during the Great Tribulation is significant.

• Christians should be aware of these developments but not live in fear.

## Key Themes

- **Human vs. Artificial Intelligence:** Human intelligence, created by God, is far more complex and spiritually enriched than artificial intelligence, which is limited by human programming.
- **AI and Morality:** AI lacks intrinsic moral values and can be programmed for good or evil, raising concerns about its potential misuse in society.
- **AI in Biblical Prophecy:** The chapter explores the possibility that AI could play a role in the end times, particularly in the deception and control prophesied to occur during the Great Tribulation.
- **Implanted Intelligence:** There are ongoing experiments to implant AI into human brains, which could revolutionize learning but also pose significant ethical and control issues.
- **Christian Perspective on AI:** Christians should understand the potential of AI while trusting in God's ultimate control and protection, especially regarding the prophesied events of the apocalypse.

## Conclusion

While AI continues to advance rapidly, its potential misuse during the end times should not cause fear among Christians. The Bible assures believers of God's sovereignty and protection. As technology progresses, Christians should remain informed and steadfast in their faith, knowing that their future is secure in God's hands.

## CHAPTER 10

# TRANSHUMANISM, CRYONICS, AND ETERNAL LIFE

### Bible Verse

"For as the body without the spirit is dead, so faith without works is dead also." - James 2:26

### Introduction

This chapter delves into the concepts of transhumanism and cryonics, exploring humanity's age-old quest for eternal life. It recounts the author's childhood fascination with baseball and a notable experience with Ted Williams, whose body was cryonically preserved, reflecting the modern pursuit of life extension through advanced technology.

### Word of Wisdom

*"True eternal life is only found through Jesus Christ, not through the promises of science."* Larry Ollison

## Main Theme

The chapter examines the philosophical, ethical, and spiritual implications of transhumanism and cryonics, contrasting them with the biblical promise of eternal life through Jesus Christ.

## Key Points

• Transhumanism advocates enhancing human conditions through technology to achieve longevity and cognition.

• The quest for eternal life is an inherent human desire, evident in historical and modern pursuits.

• Mind uploading proposes transferring human consciousness to digital storage, raising ethical debates.

• CERN's research aims to uncover the universe's mysteries, with some fearing catastrophic consequences.

• Cryonics involves freezing bodies with the hope of future revival, though it remains speculative science fiction.

• The Bible asserts that true eternal life is through Jesus, not technological means.

## Key Themes

- **Transhumanism and Eternal Life:** Transhumanism seeks to enhance human life using technology, but it ultimately aims for a posthuman existence, contrasting with the biblical view of eternal life through Jesus.
- **Cryonics and Its Challenges:** Cryonics involves preserving bodies at low temperatures, hoping for future revival, but it raises questions about the soul, spirit, and the actual feasibility of such technology.
- **Mind Uploading and Human Identity:** The concept of mind uploading suggests transferring human consciousness to computers, sparking debates on whether it enhances or diminishes human identity.
- **CERN's Mysteries and Implications:** CERN's advanced research, including particle accelerators, aims to uncover the universe's secrets, but its potential dangers and true purpose remain subjects of speculation and concern.
- **Biblical Perspective on Eternal Life:** The Bible teaches that eternal life is a gift from God through faith in Jesus Christ, offering a promise of a glorified, resurrected body that transcends human technological attempts at immortality.

## Conclusion

The chapter concludes that while transhumanism and cryonics represent humanity's desire to overcome death, true eternal life is found only through Jesus Christ. Christians are encouraged to trust in God's promise of eternal life and not be swayed by technological promises of immortality

## CHAPTER 11

## FLAT EARTH THEORY

**Bible Verse**
"It is He who sits above the circle of the earth, and its inhabitants are like grasshoppers, who stretches out the heavens like a curtain, and spreads them out like a tent to dwell in." - Isaiah 40:22

**Introduction**

The chapter explores the resurgence of the flat earth theory, a belief that the earth is flat and not a rotating globe. This idea, despite modern scientific evidence, persists in some circles and has gained a cult-like status with the rise of the Internet and social media.

**Word of Wisdom**

*"Belief or non-belief in a flat earth does not determine your salvation. Your eternal life is determined by one thing only*

*—your belief in Jesus Christ as your Lord and Savior." Larry Ollison*

## Main Theme

The chapter examines the historical, scientific, and biblical perspectives on the flat earth theory, ultimately affirming the scientific consensus that the earth is a sphere.

## Key Points

• The flat earth theory proposes that the earth is a flat disc, not a sphere.

• Historical figures and societies, like Samuel Rowbotham and the International Flat Earth Research Society, have promoted this theory.

• The theory includes variations, such as the earth being surrounded by an ice wall or existing inside a holographic dome.

• The flat earth theory has gained traction in modern times through the Internet and social media.

• Scientific evidence from Aristotle to modern astronauts confirms the earth is a sphere.

• Biblical scriptures used to support the flat earth theory are often taken out of context and do not explicitly state the earth's shape.

## Key Themes

- **Historical Context:** The flat earth theory has been advocated by various historical figures and societies, reflecting a persistent fascination with this idea despite advancements in science.
- **Modern Resurgence:** The theory has gained a renewed following due to the spread of information and misinformation on the Internet and social media platforms.
- **Scientific Evidence:** From ancient philosophers like Aristotle to modern astronauts, scientific evidence overwhelmingly supports the earth as a spherical planet.
- **Biblical Interpretation:** Scriptures cited by flat earth proponents are often misinterpreted, as the Bible neither explicitly supports nor refutes the earth's shape.
- **Focus on Faith:** Christians should not let the flat earth debate distract them from their faith in Jesus Christ, as salvation depends on belief in Him, not on scientific theories about the earth's shape.

## Conclusion

The flat earth theory, while intriguing and historically persistent, does not hold up against modern scientific evidence. Christians are encouraged to focus on their faith in Jesus Christ rather than get sidetracked by such theories. True salvation comes from confessing Jesus as Lord and believing in His resurrection.

## CHAPTER 12

## GHOSTS

### Bible Verse

"Beloved, do not imitate what is evil, but what is good. He who does good is of God, but he who does evil has not seen God." - 3 John 11

### Introduction

The chapter addresses the topic of ghosts, exploring whether they truly exist and what the Bible says about them. It differentiates between modern conceptions of ghosts and biblical teachings on spirits.

### Word of Wisdom

*"Ghosts, as defined in current vernacular through theater, movies, and novels, do not exist. But angels, both of God and fallen, do exist and there are*

*many biblical accounts of them being seen by natural eyes." Larry Ollison*

## Main Theme

The chapter asserts that while popular culture promotes the idea of ghosts as disembodied human spirits, the Bible does not support this view. Instead, spiritual manifestations are attributed to angels or demons.

## Key Points

• Popular culture defines ghosts as disembodied human spirits with unfinished business.

• The Bible uses the term "ghost" interchangeably with "spirit" (pneuma) but does not support the existence of human spirits lingering on earth.

• Demonic beings or angels may be mistaken for ghosts in reported sightings.

• Christians should avoid engaging in activities like séances that attempt to contact the dead.

• The Bible provides clear warnings against seeking guidance from mediums or familiar spirits.

• True spiritual discernment and guidance come from the Holy Spirit.

## Key Themes

- **Biblical Understanding of Spirits:** The Bible teaches that human spirits go to Hades or Paradise upon death, not lingering on earth. Demons and angels are real and can manifest, often being mistaken for ghosts.
- **Misinterpretation of Scripture:** Passages like Matthew 14:26, where Jesus' disciples think they see a ghost, are often misinterpreted. The term "ghost" in the Bible refers to spirit beings, not disembodied human spirits.
- **Dangers of Spiritual Practices:** Engaging in séances and attempting to communicate with the dead are condemned in the Bible. These practices invite demonic activity and deception.
- **Role of Demons and Angels:** Sightings of supposed ghosts are more likely encounters with demons or, less commonly, angels. Demonic spirits can deceive and frighten people, appearing as ghosts.
- **Spiritual Discernment:** Christians are gifted with the Holy Spirit, who provides discernment to identify spirits. Seeking the Holy Spirit's guidance ensures protection from deception and fear.

## Conclusion

The chapter concludes that while spirits do exist, they are either angels or demons, not disembodied human souls. Christians should rely on the Holy

Spirit for discernment and avoid practices that attempt to contact the dead. Understanding these truths helps believers avoid deception and fear, focusing instead on their faith in God

## CHAPTER 13

## WHAT IS THE MULTIVERSE?

### Bible Verse

"While we do not look at the things which are seen, but at the things which are not seen. For the things which are seen are temporary, but the things which are not seen are eternal." - 2 Corinthians 4:18

### Introduction

The chapter explores the concept of the multiverse from both a secular and Christian perspective, discussing theories about multiple universes and dimensions, and how these ideas relate to biblical teachings about the heavens and the unseen spiritual realm.

### Word of Wisdom

*"The Bible makes no reference to multiple universes, but is clear that multiple dimensions exist, and it is from the*

*unseen dimension of heaven that miracles are seen on earth." Larry Ollison*

## Main Theme

The chapter examines the idea of the multiverse, highlighting that while secular theories suggest multiple infinite universes or dimensions, the Bible supports the existence of multiple dimensions within God's creation.

## Key Points

• The Bible references multiple layers of heaven, suggesting a multi-dimensional existence.

• Secular definitions of the multiverse include various hypothetical universes containing all space, time, matter, and laws of physics.

• There are two main theories about the multiverse: infinite simultaneous universes and one universe with multiple dimensions.

• The Bible describes an unseen spiritual world influencing the physical realm.

• Miracles often involve interactions between seen and unseen dimensions.

• Spiritual discernment is necessary to understand the nature of supernatural occurrences.

## Key Themes

- **Biblical Dimensions:** The Bible indicates the existence of multiple dimensions, with references to different heavens and unseen realms influencing the physical world.
- **Secular Multiverse Theories:** The idea of infinite simultaneous universes is considered unprovable and paradoxical, while the concept of one universe with multiple dimensions aligns more closely with biblical teachings.
- **Unseen Influences:** The Bible describes how spoken words and actions in the physical realm can impact the unseen spiritual dimension, leading to real-world effects and miracles.
- **Discerning Spirits:** The Holy Spirit provides the gift of discerning spirits, enabling Christians to differentiate between true miracles from God and deceptive works from the enemy.
- **Altered Physics and Miracles:** Biblical accounts, such as Jesus appearing in a locked room, illustrate how God's power can alter physical laws, demonstrating the interaction between dimensions.

## Conclusion

While secular theories about the multiverse remain speculative and unprovable, the Bible affirms the existence of multiple dimensions, with the unseen spiritual realm playing a significant role in the physical world. Christians are encouraged to rely on the Holy Spirit for discernment and to recognize that true miracles glorify God and come from His divine power.

## CHAPTER 14

## CLIMATE CHANGE

### Bible Verse
"While the earth remains, seedtime and harvest, cold and heat, winter and summer, and day and night shall not cease." - Genesis 8:22

### Introduction

The chapter explores the contentious issue of climate change, contrasting the fears and beliefs surrounding it with biblical teachings that emphasize God's control over the earth's destiny. The discussion focuses on the balance between environmental responsibility and trust in God's promises.

### Word of Wisdom

*"Although we know the earth is aging (Hebrews 1:10-12), we should not allow fear to cause us to make foolish and*

*bizarre decisions that affect our lifestyle and restrict us from living the abundant life promised to us in the Word of God (John 10:10)."*

## Main Theme

The chapter addresses the modern controversy of climate change, highlighting the need for a balanced perspective that acknowledges environmental stewardship while trusting in God's ultimate control over the earth.

## Key Points

• The fear of climate change has been politicized and driven by various exaggerated claims.

• Historical climate changes have been dramatic and natural, predating modern human influence.

• Predictions of climate catastrophe, like those of an imminent ice age or extreme warming, have often proven incorrect.

• The Bible reassures that the earth will continue to function with its natural cycles until God's ordained end.

• Environmental responsibility is important, but it should be grounded in faith rather than fear.

• God will ultimately renew the earth after the millennial reign of Jesus.

## Key Themes

- **Historical Climate Change:** Throughout history, the earth's climate has naturally fluctuated, experiencing periods of both warming and cooling long before modern human activity.
- **Fear and Manipulation:** The fear surrounding climate change is often politically motivated and can lead to irrational behaviors and policies. It is crucial to differentiate between genuine environmental concern and fear-based manipulation.
- **Biblical Assurance:** The Bible provides assurance that the earth will continue its natural cycles of seasons and climate until God's planned renewal. This perspective helps mitigate undue fear about the future.
- **Environmental Stewardship:** Christians are called to responsibly care for the earth, avoiding harmful pollutants and maintaining the environment. This stewardship is part of our duty but should not be driven by fear.
- **God's Ultimate Control:** The chapter emphasizes that God is in control of the earth's destiny. Despite human concerns about climate change, the Bible assures that the earth will remain until God's appointed time for renewal.

## Conclusion

While environmental stewardship is important, Christians should not be overwhelmed by fear regarding climate change. The Bible assures that the earth will continue its natural cycles until God's planned renewal. Trust in God's control should guide our actions and alleviate fears about the future.

## CHAPTER 15

## HEAVEN, HELL, AND ETERNITY

**Bible Verse**

"He has made everything beautiful in its time. Also He has put eternity in their hearts, except that no one can find out the work that God does from beginning to end." - Ecclesiastes 3:11

**Introduction**

This chapter explores the concepts of heaven, hell, and eternity from a Christian perspective, detailing their descriptions, purposes, and the conditions for accessing each. It contrasts these biblical views with those of other religions and emphasizes the choices that determine one's eternal destination.

**Word of Wisdom**

*"Your eternal existence is determined and established while you are living on the earth in your flesh-and-blood body before*

*death or the catching away of the church." Larry Ollison*

## Main Theme

The chapter elucidates the Christian understanding of heaven, hell, and eternity, emphasizing the reality of these places and the importance of making choices in this life that affect one's eternal destiny.

## Key Points

• Heaven is a real, beautiful place created by God for the eternal enjoyment of the righteous.

• There are multiple dimensions and areas within heaven, including Paradise and the heavenly Jerusalem.

• Hell is a place of eternal punishment created for Satan and his followers, also serving as the destination for those who reject Christ.

• The concept of eternity in the Bible describes a realm without beginning or end, where God exists beyond time.

• Eternal life or eternal punishment is determined by one's relationship with Jesus Christ.

• God's love and justice necessitate the existence of heaven and hell, with each serving distinct purposes in the divine plan.

## Key Themes

- **Heaven's Multi-Dimensional Nature:** Heaven is described as a multi-dimensional realm with areas like Paradise and the heavenly Jerusalem, reflecting its vastness and complexity.
- **The Heavenly City - New Jerusalem:** After the millennium, the heavenly Jerusalem will be refurbished and descend upon the earthly Jerusalem, becoming the New Jerusalem, the eternal home of the saints.
- **The Reality of Hell:** Hell is a literal place of eternal torment, described in vivid detail in the Bible, created for Satan and his angels, and for those who reject Jesus.
- **Eternity Defined:** Eternity is described as an infinite, unending realm where God's presence encapsulates the universe, and the eternal existence of humans is determined by their choices in this life.
- **The Importance of Choice:** The chapter emphasizes the significance of choosing life and accepting Jesus Christ as Lord and Savior, as this choice determines one's eternal destiny.

## Conclusion

The chapter concludes by reiterating that the choices made in this life have eternal consequences. The decision to accept or reject Jesus Christ determines whether one spends eternity in the glory of heaven or the torment of hell. God's love and justice provide the framework for these realities, urging believers to choose wisely and share the message of salvation with others.

## CHAPTER 16

# THE MYSTERY OF THE HEBREW LANGUAGE

**Bible Verse**

"In the beginning was the Word, and the Word was with God, and the Word was God." - John 1:1

**Introduction**

This chapter explores the divine nature and unique characteristics of the Hebrew language, emphasizing its role in the Bible as a prophetic book. The Hebrew language is presented as multidimensional, encoded with mysteries, and integral to God's communication with humanity.

**Word of Wisdom**

*"The Hebrew language is unchanging and eternal, uniquely designed by God to convey His divine messages." Larry Ollison*

## Main Theme

The Hebrew language is a divinely inspired, multidimensional medium through which God's prophetic messages are revealed, embodying mathematical, musical, and artistic elements that underscore its eternal and unchanging nature.

## Key Points

• The Hebrew Bible is filled with prophetic mysteries meant to be revealed to God's people.

• Hebrew is the language used by God in significant biblical events, such as the giving of the Ten Commandments.

• Each letter of the Hebrew alphabet has multiple dimensions, including numeric values and symbols.

• The Hebrew language was divinely designed 3,500 years ago with words that have future significance.

• Unlike other languages, Hebrew remains unchanged and eternal, akin to a digital recording.

• The precise and unchanged transmission of the Hebrew Bible over millennia demonstrates its divine preservation.

## Key Themes

- **Unique Characteristics of Hebrew:**
  Hebrew's multidimensional nature includes mathematical, musical, and artistic elements, with each letter having specific

meanings and values, indicating its divine origin.

- **Divine Preservation:** The meticulous copying of the Torah by scribes, ensuring no errors and preserving the text over centuries, highlights the divine care taken to maintain the integrity of God's Word.
- **Prophetic Significance:** The Hebrew Bible contains hidden codes and prophetic messages that are revealed over time, showcasing God's intricate plan and the supernatural accuracy of the Scriptures.
- **Musical Dimension:** Hebrew letters correspond to musical notes, creating harmonious music that has the power to soothe and repel evil, as demonstrated by King David's harp playing.
- **Aleph and Tav:** Jesus referring to Himself as the Aleph and Tav (Alpha and Omega) connects Him directly to the written Word of God from the beginning, underscoring His divine role in creation and redemption.

## Conclusion

The Hebrew language is a miraculous, divinely inspired medium that encapsulates God's prophetic messages and remains unchanged through time. Its multidimensional nature and precise preservation demonstrate its significance as a conduit for divine revelation. Embracing the mysteries of the Hebrew language deepens our understanding of God's eternal plan and His communication with humanity.

**Remember:** "In the beginning was the Word, and the Word was with God, and the Word was God." - John 1:1

Harrison House is a Spirit-filled, Word of Faith Christian publisher dedicated to spreading the message of faith, hope, and love through our wide range of inspiring publications. Committed to the messages that highlight the power of the Word and Spirit, we provide books, devotionals, and study guides that empower believers to live victorious, faith-filled lives.

Our resources are designed to help readers grow spiritually, strengthen their faith, and experience the transformative power of God's Word. Harrison House is passionate about equipping Christians with the tools they need to fulfill their divine purpose and impact the world for Christ.

www.ingramcontent.com/pod-product-compliance
Lightning Source LLC
LaVergne TN
LVHW051511070426
835507LV00022B/3054